1·85

Dublin
PORTRAIT OF A CITY

Dublin
PORTRAIT OF A CITY

PHOTOGRAPHS BY PETER ZÖLLER • TEXT BY JOSEPH McARDLE

GILL & MACMILLAN

Gill & Macmillan Ltd
Goldenbridge
Dublin 8
with associated companies throughout the world
0 7171 2538 6
© Photographs Peter Zöller 1997
© Text Joseph McArdle 1997

Design and print origination by
O'K Graphic Design, Dublin

Printed by Edelvives, Spain

A catalogue record for this book is available from the British Library.

5 4 3 2 1

I disclaim all fertile meadows, all tilled land
The evil that grows from it and the good,
But the Dublin of old statutes, this arrogant city,
Stirs proudly and secretly in my blood.

T he life of a city is a family saga: the humble beginnings, the gradual accumulation of wealth and movement up the social ladder, black sheep, saints and eccentrics, good marriages and bad, powerful connections and *mésalliances*, improvident generations squandering the capital of centuries, decline and genteel poverty leading to extinction, or the introduction of new blood to mark a new beginning. Dublin has been through them all.

Dublin may be compared to a conversation in one of its own pubs. Friends line up before their drinks at the counter; their talk sets out in a certain direction, but soon it gets sidetracked to another line of thought, which branches off again and again like a vascular diagram. The dull may get it back to its beginnings for five minutes, but free association and lateral thinking soon replace linearity. When the conversationalists stagger out into the rainy night, it is with the comforting illusion that a pattern has been followed and great questions have been settled.

The view along Westmoreland Street towards O'Connell Bridge, with the old House of Lords, now part of the Bank of Ireland, on the left

The view west at night

For over three hundred years, the city was content with the side of a hill between the Liffey and High Street. Five hundred years later, it was still only half a mile wide between its east and west gates. Then in the space of seventy-five breakneck years between 1610 and 1685, the land pushed the river back into Dublin Bay, the city burst through its old walls, and its winding lanes sprouted streets and squares to the north, west and east. The next hundred years saw the construction of Malton's iconic Dublin, now stamped on a thousand tablemats and frozen in time like St Petersburg or Edinburgh. Ship's ballast from Bristol was the brick to build Dublin's glory. Dublin craftsmen supplied the rest — the ornate doorways, the fanlights, the stone steps, iron railings and balconies, the delicate ceilings, walls and fireplaces.

Soon the twin canals became the city's moat and the centre of gravity dropped south. But when political power shifted to London after the Act of Union (1800) and economic power was handed over to the Catholic middle classes, the city sank into a long decline. Dublin had always fed on the flight of the prosperous from the proximity of the poor. Now the professional classes moved to Donnybrook, Ranelagh, Ballsbridge and Clontarf, while the poor squeezed into their abandoned houses and died in the famines of the 1820s and 1840s. Kingstown, Dalkey and Killiney became fashionable in their turn. Slum clearance in the 1930s gave birth to Cabra, Drimnagh, Marino, Donnycarney, Ballyfermot — dreary and monotonous one-class areas, lacking character or identity. As Kathleen Behan, Brendan's mother, put it:

> All of us slum-dwellers thought that when de Valera came into power he would put boots on the footless . . . but it all turned out very different. He built those great housing estates, like something you'd see in Siberia. It was a terrible thing to move half the city out on to the sides of the mountains, without schools, buses or shops . . . in the slums we lived a rebellious, anarchic life that didn't suit the new Ireland at all.

Between 1958 and 1975, peripheral expansion continued in a 'commodious *vicus*' of recirculation from Killiney to Howth. The first and last high-rise towers rose in Ballymun. With populations greater than many provincial towns, Tallaght, Blanchardstown and Clondalkin became wastelands to the west.

And that's where the family stands today: a few very rich, many struggling to pay their mortgages, and many many more across the ocean or on the dole. The crack was mighty tonight, but we'll wake up in the morning.

The dome of the Custom House in silhouette

Under the pillars of the General Post Office in O'Connell Street

A street scene on Aston's Quay

Inside Kilmainham prison, where the leaders of the 1916 Rising were held prior to execution

As I walked down through Dublin City
At the hour of twelve in the night,
Who should I spy but a Spanish Lady
Washing her feet by candle-light?
First she dipped them, then she dried them
Over a fire of ambery coal.
In all my life I ne'r did see
A maid so neat about the sole.

It is impossible to paint Dublin without preconceived emotions and associations. When we walk along the Grand Canal and imagine Patrick Kavanagh sitting on his bench by the frothing lock, or visit Portobello Harbour and conjure up flyboats arriving from Monasterevin, we are pilgrims and earn grace by standing in the spot where these things took place. We are brought closer to the events, but the superimposition of the past on the present can blind us to the latter. A guidebook helps, but it also distracts. Ideally, a city should be visited twice, once in a state of primal innocence. The study of statistics and trivia should take place at home or in a hotel bedroom and, with this imperfect knowledge, one is equipped for the imaginative time-travel and intellectual understanding that is the reward of a new environment.

Getting to know a city should be like a holiday romance. In the beginning, the eyes are everything, they send signals and look for clues, they record the first impression powerfully and the second or third more critically. It is only when they say 'Yes' that names and background are exchanged.

I know my love by his way of walking,
And I know my love by his way of talking,
And I know my love dressed in his jersey blue,
And if my love leaves me, what will I do?

In 1840 two travel writers, Mr and Mrs Hall, advised the visitor to stand 'nearly in the centre of the city upon Carlisle Bridge [now O'Connell Bridge]' because 'from no single spot can the eye command so great a number of interesting points'. This is still a good vantage point.

The Old Library in Trinity College which houses the Book of Kells

Marsh's Library, near St Patrick's Cathedral, is one of the city's hidden treasures.

Greene's Book Shop in Clare Street is a Dublin institution.

To the north, O'Connell Street is a wide avenue intersected by statues and trees; to the south, pedestrians and motor traffic jerk down Westmoreland Street and curl around College Green and Trinity railings. The right is all sea and sky: an east wind blows on your face, you listen for the cries of the scavenging gulls over the squeals and grumbles of buses and lorries, you note the tower of Liberty Hall, and peep under the vandalising railway bridge to glimpse the Custom House and the glassy Financial Services Centre. Down west along the quays, bridges link north and south: the Four Courts and St Michan's to Adam and Eve's and the Municipal Buildings. At this spot you can sniff the river and the sea, fried food from the Abrakebabra beside the Ballast Office, inhale petrol and diesel. You are in a no-man's-land where northside and southside meet.

Dublin lies on a gentle rise from the seashore to the higher northern ground and the southern hills, with modest valleys sloping down to the Liffey, the Dodder and the Tolka. It is 'particularly fortunate in its surroundings', wrote Weston St John Joyce in *The Neighbourhoods of Dublin*; 'Within easy reach lies an attractive coast where in close association may be found cliff, beach and towering headland. On the south a great mountain tract provides an almost endless variety of moorland, valley and river scenery.'

A picture of the city can begin with the general — a flight over Dublin Bay circling above

Lambay Island and Ireland's Eye, the crab's claw of Howth Head, the sands of the Bull Island, the stripe of the Liffey, the pincers of the harbours, Dalkey Island, Killiney Strand, Bray Head and the Sugar Loaf mountain; or with the particular — a close-up of South Richmond Street along Lennox Street past the Bretzel Bakery and the Jewish Museum to Bloomfield Avenue, where Chaim Herzog, President of Israel, grew up, and across the South Circular Road to Lombard Street West where Molly and Leopold Bloom were happy. It is hard to imagine that these quiet redbrick streets, with their unique pattern of 'artisan dwellings', are only ten minutes' walk from the heart of a capital city.

The general and the particular can be combined in a long pan along dual carriageways flanked by factories with German, Japanese and American names, or streeling avenues running north and south across the two canals. This is best done on a Sunday or in the early morning; otherwise, lines of traffic will obstruct the view.

An interior in Newman House on St Stephen's Green

13

View looking west along the Liffey with the Ha'penny Bridge in the forefront and Guinness's Brewery in the background

The new civic offices on Wood Quay are a worthy addition to the city's river-front architecture.

Sunlight House on the south quays

16

On this early morning incursion, you will not meet the tunnels, the raging motorways and the menacing phalanxes of overbearing tower blocks that, like the tangled forest protecting the Sleeping Beauty, have sprung up around the city centres of France, Spain or Italy. You will follow the progress of fields, housing estates and shopping centres, residential roads where gardens exchange their high walls for Victorian railings, roads becoming streets as houses draw together and gardens disappear, the gradual triumph of shops and supermarkets, and the final victory of offices, government buildings and the great stores, the whole punctuated by churches and public houses. You will note the bewildering diversity of the houses: the pebble dash villas of the 1930s; the 'period' private estates; the council estates thrown up around a tired open space with no soft areas, their winding roads without vegetation or accessible street signs, their ironic parks, drives, crescents and avenues named after absent trees or English shires; four-storey aristocrats among houses with sloping front gardens; cottages with embroidered aprons of flowers; and new flats availing of tax concessions. Within the cordon of housing estates, private or public, every dwelling cries out its individuality. Each door has its own colour and its own distinctive knocker. Some doors have glass porches, some windows have aluminium frames. There are cars on the asphalt where once there was a lawn. A house is protected by old trees and new flowers: please, don't look at the rows of bells, pinned like ribbons of shame to the door frame. Once it sheltered a single family. Now students and office workers live in separate rooms and take the bus home to Kerry or Roscommon every weekend. There was a time when these brass plates were the *sine qua non* of a gentleman's residence. These days the floors creak under the burden of computers and fax machines.

Later in the day you can sketch the vivacity of the enclosed souks of the ILAC Centre, the Grafton Centre or Powerscourt Town House, and guess at the subtle differences between northsiders and southsiders. Perhaps these are only apparent to the natives. Much of the display in the shop windows of the centre city streets — Grafton Street, Dawson Street, Nassau Street, O'Connell Street, Henry Street, Talbot Street — is international. The old names — Weirs, Arnotts, Kennys, Boylans, Brown Thomas, Cassidys, Hayes Conyngham & Robinson, Clerys — are being edged out.

Wander through the narrow lanes behind the Four Courts, the vegetable and cattle markets where dehydrated drinkers can find pubs with early morning licence to open for the market workers at hours when ordinary pubs are still shut.

The Ha'penny Bridge joins the northside of the river to Merchant's Arch, leading to Temple Bar.

Lucan, Co. Dublin, looking across the Liffey

Old and new

The Gaelic names of Dublin's former villages, Baldoyle (*Baile Dubh Gall* — The Town of the Dark Strangers, the Danes), Chapelizod (*Séipéil Izod* — the Chapel of Iseult), Clontarf (*Cluain Tarbh* — the Meadow of the Bull), Coolock (*An Cúlóg* — The Little Corner), Crumlin (*Cruimghlinn* — The Crooked Glen), Donnycarney (*Domhnach Cearnach* — The Church of Cearnach), Finglas (*Fionn Glas* — The Clear Stream), Santry (*Sean Triabh* — The Old Tribe), Tallaght (*Tamhlacht* — The plague grave 'of a colony from Greece!') should be contrasted with the un-Gaelic of Werburgh Street, Paradise Place, Rialto, Dolphin's Barn, Portobello, Pump-Alley Street, Marino, Essex Quay, Protestant Row and Fishamble Street, to show how the 'misfortunate' Dubliners were hemmed in by the wild Irish from beyond the Pale.

Says my oul' wan to your oul' wan
We have no beef or mutton
But if we go down to Monto Town
We might get drink for nuttin'
Here's a piece of advice
I got from an oul' fishmonger
When food is scarce and you see the hearse
You'll know you've died of hunger.

The introduction of a kitchen sink to an art gallery compels the public to look at it out of context and therefore see it. Shuttered houses off Dorset Street, 'troughs of slumland, bleak wastes disfigured by huge advertising billboards hiding half-hidden or demolished buildings' — all are as much Dublin as the elegant southside squares. In the 1970s the centre of the city had been so ravaged by speculators and its own Corporation that it was compared unfavourably to the bombed-out cities of Europe in the late 1940s, and described as 'a great beauty wrapped in a tattered shawl'. In many of those continental cities, shattered treasures have, as an act of piety, been painstakingly restored brick by brick and stone by stone and no one complains that they are pastiche or fake. In Samarkand, mosques and madrassahs have been returned to their former beauty and one thanks God for the skill of the Soviet craftsmen. But in Dublin there has been an ongoing dispute for thirty years over restoration, reproduction and pastiche, and the danger of a neo-Georgian Disneyland. In the last five to ten years, there have been brand new buildings, but too many of them, all clock towers and pretty turrets, look for all the world like Lego.

Some years ago a battle was fought and lost to prevent a multi-lane highway being built from the South Circular Road to Christ Church Cathedral. Traffic congestion has not

In the Liberties

Among Temple Bar's many attractions is the Ark, a children's theatre with a reversible stage which can be used for plays in the theatre or outside, as here.

diminished, but the rat-infested ruins have gone and, if you have money, you can buy an elegant apartment overlooking St Patrick's Park as continental as they come.

Have you heard of one Humpty Dumpty
How he fell with a roll and a rumble
And curled up like Lord Olofa Crumple
By the butt of the Magazine Wall,
Hump, helmet and all?

Change in cities takes many forms. Rivers, as in the case of both Liffey and Dodder, are corseted by walls or, like the Poddle, buried underground. Roads are widened and narrowed. But most affecting is the removal of old landmarks.

If ever there was an icon of Dublin, the equivalent of the Eiffel Tower in Paris, it had to be Nelson Pillar, a doric column built in 1808. There must be some reason why in London a similar erection is called 'Nelson's Column' but in Dublin was always 'the Pillar'. In 1966, the fiftieth anniversary of the Easter Rising, an IRA bomb neatly removed the top half of the column without causing any surrounding damage. The *coup de grâce* explosion, carried out by army engineers two days later, smashed most of the windows in O'Connell Street.

This unlucky explosion was the signal for an orgy of destruction. For almost twenty years, building after building, beloved of Dubliners, disappeared: the Capitol Cinema; the Metropole Cinema; the Theatre Royal in Hawkins Street, with its 'exterior in art deco style and a richly lavish Moorish architectural scheme for the auditorium . . . based on authentic details from the Alhambra at Granada in Spain', which offered a variety act with the Royalettes and Eddie Byrne; Tommy Dando on 'the largest and most modern theatre organ yet built'; shorts and a feature film. The old Jurys Hotel in Dame Street went. So did the Dolphin and the legendary Jammets restaurant. The 'Four Pros' dancehall was replaced by Swedish offices. One side of Molesworth Street came tumbling down, as did the interior of the Kildare Street Club. Down came Hume Street, the wonderful Irish House on Wood Quay, Wesley College, the Russell Hotel, most of St Stephen's Green West, the Swiss Chalet, the Turkish Baths in Lincoln Place, the Queen's Theatre in Pearse Street, Leopold Bloom's house at No. 7 Eccles Street. Why go on?

Broadstone and Harcourt Street stations have been converted to profane usage. Robert Lynd wrote that Ruskin would surely have been surprised if he had been told that a time

The Abbey Theatre

Central Bank Plaza on Dame Street

One of the city's classic Georgian views, looking along Upper Mount Street towards the 'Pepper Canister' Church

would come when the closing of an old railway station would move men to sadness no less than the demolition of a Gothic church or the violation of a landscape. What would he have made of the transformation of Harcourt Street Station into the POD night-club and the Chocolate Bar?

Lynd captures such loss precisely:

> Life is brief, and the removal of a long-tolerated equally with a long-loved landmark alters and injures the world in which we have been happier than we have deserved to be. . . . If you have tears to shed, then, spare a few of them for Broadstone Station. Without it — for better or for worse — Dublin will never be the same again.

To understand Dublin today, one must take these upheavals into account and remember that they followed a period of stagnation during which, in one five-year period in the 1950s,

> nearly half a million men and women left Ireland convinced that it was doomed, and unwilling to suffer any further torments that the Irish bourgeoisie might devise for those who remained behind. Many of them went with a new understanding that this time the guilty men were not 'British Imperialists' but their own fellow countrymen.

The decorative sculpture of Edward Smyth adorns the roof of the Custom House.

It was a period in which revolutionaries exchanged their guns for Homburgs and a chance to kiss the Papal Nuncio's ring; when the Stalinist Garden of Remembrance was constructed in Parnell Square; when Lutyens's melancholy memorial garden on the banks of the Liffey at Islandbridge — commemorating the Irishmen who died in the Great War — was neglected; when emigration, censorship and Church-influenced legislation confirmed a corporate state and congealed everything to such an extent that the Victorian and Edwardian atmosphere of *Ulysses* was still familiar fifty years after the first Bloomsday. But not any more. All is now changed utterly, and the rough beast slouching to be born is a terrible ignorance of the past.

> *She died of the fever*
> *And no one could save her,*
> *And that was the end of sweet Molly Malone.*
> *But her ghost wheels her barrow,*
> *Through streets broad and narrow,*
> *Crying, 'Cockles and mussels, alive, alive, oh!'*

A view from the new civic offices on Wood Quay

The Financial Services Centre at Memorial Road is one of the city's most pleasing modern buildings. In the background is Busáras dating from 1953, which was regarded as revolutionary in its day.

This is no plea to live in the past. Tom Kettle defended his power to abandon old things like this: 'The whole world is nothing but the story of a renegade. The bud is renegade to the tree, and the flower to the bud, and the fruit to the flower.' Life was a sustained goodbye, he said, 'a cheap *table d'hôte* in a rather dirty restaurant, with Time changing the plates before you have had enough of anything', but, as a philosopher, he bewailed the necessity of change and proposed that only death would grant us our ideal of going away and going home at the same time. Kettle left for home a few years later on the Somme.

We need change yet we deplore it, but it is not so much the absence of landmarks as the changes in ourselves that we mourn. How many students who pawned their textbooks in Merediths of Cuffe Street and then spent the money on a pint of rough cider in the Winter Garden Palace are now Assistant Secretaries in the Civil Service? How many teetotallers passing the archway of the Grafton Gallery remember Christmas Eves celebrated unwisely in the old Royal Hibernian Hotel? How can the consultant in Guy's forget the night that his landlady in Leeson Street banged on his locked door to ask if he was entertaining and he replied, 'Hold on and I'll ask.'

> *Margaret, are you grieving*
> *Over Goldengrove unleaving? . . .*
> *It is the blight man was for born for,*
> *It is Margaret you mourn for.*

A picture of Dublin would be incomplete without mentioning the face-lift that never happened. 'Nature has given you a winning hand,' Lord Leverhulme said to Dublin in 1911; 'all that Nature asks is that you play the game.' The inheritors of the city took him at his word and in 1922 planned to create a new civic centre between Green Street and Capel Street with an underground rail system throughout the city, and then create a new 'Place de la Concorde' stretching from Little Britain Street to Upper Ormond Quay. Tree-lined boulevards would run along the north side of the Liffey. At the head of Capel Street, behind the King's Inns, the new National Cathedral would dominate the city.

And things have improved (in the southside at least). Special tax zones have been introduced which have caused huge capital sums to be invested in the run-down areas where buddleia once sprouted from crumbling brick walls wherever one turned.

The chip has dropped from the Irish shoulder and, whatever their historical

The statue of the historian W. E. H. Lecky, in Trinity College, with accessory

Grafton Street teems with life. It is Dublin's most fashionable street.

Outside Bewley's of Grafton Street

Cyclists

reverberations, the symbols of Ascendancy triumphalism have been made 'part of what we are', the great stone public buildings have been cleaned up, their settings have been improved and their uses have been adapted to present needs. (In fairness, it must be admitted that there are still many 'Royal' societies and institutions in Dublin and, under the green paint, many pillar boxes are still stamped 'VR'.) Government Buildings in Upper Merrion Street has a French imperial splendour. The transformation from University College Dublin to the National Concert Hall in Earlsfort Terrace has been successful. Winetavern Street may no longer be a picturesque huddle of redbrick ruins and a market for second-hand clothes, but the new chambers, covered with creepers, are already beginning to mellow.

Most of Dublin is brighter, cleaner and healthier than it has been for two hundred years. Go tell the barristers in the Shelbourne's Horseshoe Bar, the diners in Patrick Gilbaud's or the swells in Ailesbury Road that 'conventional Irish pleasures do not include eating well or dressing smartly or living in nicely designed rooms' and see what dusty answers you will get. Grafton Street may have slid down-market to become a cheap imitation of 'a second-class street in any English provincial town', but it is the street they pour into when the sun shines and, on Christmas Eve when the emigrant graduates are home from London, Düsseldorf, Paris, New York and Boston, it is like a street-long party in Emer's and Gavin's place in Hampstead.

In a city where night-life was the legend of Dolly Fossets or red wine poured surreptitiously from a teapot, first-class restaurants proliferate — Chinese, French, Indian, Italian, Japanese, Mexican, Russo-Finnish, even Irish. And they are always full!

I'm a buxom fine widow, I live in a spot,
In Dublin they call it the Coombe;
My shops and my stalls are laid out on the street,
And my palace consists of one room.
I sell apples and oranges, nuts and split peas,
Bananas and sugar-stick sweet,
On Saturday night I sell second-hand clothes
From the floor of my stall on the street.

Like 'Biddy Mulligan, the Pride of the Coombe', the song 'Dublin in the rare oul' times' has achieved ballad status and there is an industry in books about the Liberties which

South Anne Street links Grafton Street and Dawson Street. The view is enclosed by St Anne's Church.

Moore Street market, the bustling, noisy street market near O'Connell Street

complain that there are no 'characters' nowadays, while canonising the street characters of the past — Bang Bang, the Bird Kavanagh, Zozimus, Endymion. 'Oh, he's a great character' often means that he's a drunken lout who will perform on cue for a drink or a cigarette and should be avoided like the plague. This Dublin need for 'characters' springs from a view of street life as a continual *commedia dell'arte* performance. When character actors appeared on screen in Dublin's beloved Hollywood films of the thirties and forties, the audience knew on cue whether to hiss, laugh or to feel their skin creep. Dublin street characters were (and are) condemned to play the same role again and again for citizen and visitor. Their life is a public one, as vendors, musicians or religious fanatics. They are part of the streetscape like the statues or the pigeons. They are usually poor and more often than not a little crazed. They play the same role for the general populace that jesters and fools played in royal courts. Nowadays, together with the doors of Dublin, their photographs are printed on posters to sell the city.

But, like the Irish bull, there is a logic in the illogicality of this elevation of the anti-social. Oliver St John Gogarty, commenting on the humour of Dublin jarveys, wrote that he had always taken it with a grain of salt, suspicious that it was marketed for tourists who came prepared to see fun in anything Irish. Then one day, he understood it. A group of 'chisellers' (otherwise 'youngsters') were watching the men on the Guinness barges as they cast off with a solemnity more suited to a trip to Valparaiso than Athy. 'Hey, misther,' shouted one boy, 'bring us back a parrot!'

If London is an imperial ode printed on a souvenir mug in the tackier end of Oxford Street, Washington a national anthem, Vienna a waltz played by a military band, Paris a roll of alexandrines backed by an accordion, Dublin is a street ballad bringing great events down to earth with a bump and reaffirming the singer by drowning his sorrows in sentimentality.

And eccentricity had its own reasons, as in the case of old Johnnie Fox of Bride Street. He had a balcony built up near the ceiling, with no stairs up to it, and a big chair in which he sat surrounded by shelves and boxes of all sorts, and a big fishing net in his hand. A customer would call out, 'A twist of shag, John', and down would come the net with the tobacco and up would go threepence. 'Why does he do that, Da?' a little boy asked his father one day. 'Why, son, there is not a process-server in Dublin can get at him with notice to quit.'

Dubliner

The Campanile in Trinity

The Custom House, completed in 1791, is probably the finest building of Dublin's golden age.

A Christmas turkey

*One-man band in
Duke Street*

44

She is far from the land where her young hero sleeps,
And lovers are round her sighing,
But coldly she turns from the gaze and weeps,
For her heart in his grave is lying!

As in everything else, Dublin's history is in its songs. 'Bold Robert Emmet', 'Kevin Barry' and 'Tipperary so far away' are songs of defeat and rebellion. 'Courtin' in the Kitchen' recalls the big houses around St Stephen's Green and the Repeal of the Union agitation. 'The Finding of Moses' keeps the memory of the old balladeers alive. 'Cockles and Mussels' celebrates street trading in fish or in flesh and the perennial filth, fever and famine of the slums, 'Dicey Reilly', the 'Waxies Dargle' and 'The Night before Larry was stretched' the alcoholic escape route. 'Biddy Mulligan' was a street trader too, but she was also Jimmy O'Dea, who with Harry O'Donovan, Noel Purcell, Cecil Sheridan and Maureen Potter represent music hall and pantomime and a certain heart of old Dublin that continued to beat for a very long time.

In Agypt's land, contagious to the Nile
Old Pharoah's daughter went to bathe in style.
She tuk her dip and came unto the land,
And for to dry her royal pelt she ran along the strand.
A bull-rush tripped her, whereupon she saw
A smiling babby in a wad of straw;
She took it up and said in accents mild
'Oh, tare-an-ages, girruls, which of yiz owns the child?'

An oul blackamore woman among the crew
Cried out, 'You royal savage, what's that to do with you?
Your royal ladies is too meek and miyul'
To beget dishonestly this darlin' little chiyul'.'
'Ah then,' says Pharoah, 'I'll search every nook
From the Phoenix Park down to Donnybrook
And when I catch hoult of the little bastard's father
I'll kick the bleedin' gouger from the Nile down to the Dodder.'

The Casino at Marino, originally built as a country retreat for Lord Charlemont in the 1780s

The memorial at Dun Laoghaire to lifeboat men who lost their lives

Dublin has never been a heroic city. This is not Stalingrad or Warsaw, or even Limerick or Derry. Apart from the Easter Rising of 1916 and the civil war, we need to go back to the early Middle Ages and briefly to the seventeenth century to find its citizens under siege. An English official, describing the view from his train window between Kingstown (as Dun Laoghaire was then known) and Dublin in 1912, was unfair to the archetypal diarist of the comic novel *Diary of a Nobody* when he commented, 'It all seemed Pooter country, all neat, ugly, smug and middle class', but a rapid survey of the city's history seems to prove that, throughout the thousand plus years of its existence, the city's ethos has been mainly Pooterish (the middle classes gathering enough money to put trade behind them and receive invitations to Dublin Castle) while the majority of its citizens existed in conditions which were among the worst in Europe.

The city's history began with pirates who settled down to steady respectability, a pattern that repeated itself on a number of occasions in later history. Elizabethans on the make pirated the profits of the monasteries and set themselves up in nervous provincial splendour. Later, the land confiscations throughout the country in Cromwell's time established a new class of grandees — none of them quite polished enough for England but fine for the rougher Irish margins — who formed the basis of what became the Irish Ascendancy. One of their number, Sir Jonah Barrington (1760–1834), famously divided them into three categories: half-mounted gentlemen; gentlemen every inch of them; and gentlemen to the back bone. Quite what the distinction was between the latter two groups is anyone's guess, but the half-mounted gentlemen were the down-at-heel, mortgaged, rakish squireens of literary legend.

The second half of the eighteenth century was the heyday of the Irish Ascendancy. They had their own domestic parliament on College Green — now the Bank of Ireland — and they built magnificent town houses, thus setting their stamp on the city forever in brick and stone, plaster and glass. Complete with a substratum of half-mounted bucks, bullies and bravos, the Irish peerage created the city we have inherited; then the Act of Union of 1800 shut down their parliament and fashion followed the MPs to Westminster. The town houses were abandoned, quickly turning to slums in the less fashionable parts of the city and to smug centres of bourgeois gentility elsewhere. Dublin entered its long sleep, a provincial city living on its past glories, a mixture of suffocating respectability and savage poverty. This was the city from which Bernard Shaw fled at the age of twenty, the hopelessly inert and resigned place that Joyce characterised as 'the centre of paralysis'.

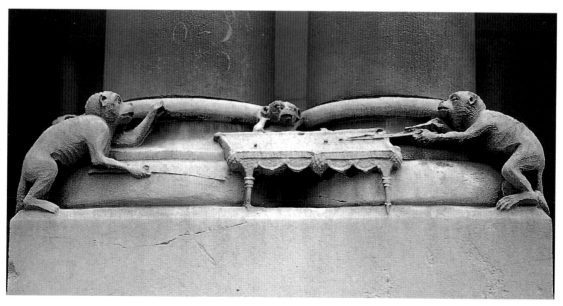

A detail on the Alliance Française building, formerly the Kildare Street Club,
at the corner of Kildare Street and Leinster Street

The old canal hotel at Portobello Bridge

The literary revival, the labour upheavals and the political revolution of the early twentieth century, all left the city shaken but not stirred. When the dust settled in the 1920s, somnolent Dublin resumed its Pooterish way until forty years later a new breed of pirate brought a rapacious energy to bear on the tired bricks of the city. In the 1960s, Lupin Pooter, the extravagant son, put on a mohair suit and became a property developer. He knocked down much that was beautiful and put up much that was ugly, but at least he brought an animal energy to the weary town. Now Dublin is run by the new bourgeoisie, almost embarrassingly European in its loyalties but at least more stylishly refined in its architectural taste. Latterly, there have been some truly distinguished buildings erected in the city, particularly at the riverine Financial Services Centre and at Temple Bar.

A steward at the Horse Show

Then we'll have a free trade Gael's brass band and mass meeting
For to sod the brave son of Scandiknavery.
And we'll bury him down in Oxmanstown
Along with the devil and Danes,
(Chorus) With the deaf and dumb Danes,
And all their remains.

Fittingly, as the capital city of a nation of emigrants, Dublin was never an Irish city in the sense that Cork, Limerick or Galway have always been. It is an English-speaking city on an island between Britain and the North American continent. The majority of the

Merrion Strand on the south shore of Dublin Bay, looking back towards the city. In the distance are the twin chimneys of the Electricity Supply Board's station at Poolbeg.

An aerial view of the Liffey Valley near Lucan. The area is known as the Strawberry Beds.

A bog road in the mountains, just above the city

writers associated with it belong to the genus 'Anglo-Irish' and, from the very beginning, its elite were not accepted in England as English. Though it keeps trying, it has not yet become American.

Norman French was replaced in Dublin by Middle English, which survived on this side of the Irish Sea long after it had been superseded in Britain. It was not, however, replaced by modern English but by an Anglo-Gaelic hybrid, which in turn spawned an amazing variety of distinctive accents for such a small city by which for many years a skilled ear could identify class, religion, age and district. Standardisation has not triumphed utterly because the past twenty years have seen the birth of a new accent among the affluent young. Its grandparents come from Sloane Square, Rathgar, the music hall stage and somewhere in mid-Atlantic. Micheál MacLiammóir is its fairy godmother. It is called 'Dortspeak' because many of those who use it live in an area of the soul called Dublin 4, along the line of the Dublin Area Rapid Transport system (the DART) and one of the characteristics of the language is to pronounce the 'a' of standard English as 'o': 'porty' for 'party, 'ort' instead of 'art'. The broad vowels have always been pure in Hiberno-English. Dortspeakers use diphthongs and umlauts as if they had invented them. An aside: travellers can read a new Poem on the DART every month as they commute to and from work.

Over seventy years into independence, the barrier of the Pale is as high as ever and, even though the vast majority of Dublin's citizens are now of rural origin, on most issues it is Dublin against the rest, the farmers against the PAYE workers, the moral majority against the 'so-called liberals'. The two-thirds who live outside Dublin often see themselves as exiled on the periphery of Ireland and Europe and claim that all the privileges of Ireland's new prosperity go to the third who live in the metropolis.

Although the episcopal crozier has over the past few years increasingly stabbed its holder in the foot, voting patterns on issues such as contraception, divorce and abortion still show a sharp divide between Dublin and the rural hinterland, and there have been sad examples of Dublin demagogues exploiting this divide for their own purposes.

When Dublin became a provincial capital, it looked to London to gauge the measure of its worth. Many of the great — Sheridan, Goldsmith, Wilde and Shaw — took the boat to Holyhead. Others, like Swift and Kavanagh, always hankered after acceptance in London. Brendan Behan was the forerunner of the new wave. He made a career in three centres: Dublin, London and New York.

Now Dublin looks beyond Britain. The Irish enthusiasm for the European Union is not only the professional interest of the beggar on O'Connell Bridge, but also a folk memory of a time when we could reach across the Berlin Wall of the intervening island and deal on equal terms with people and cultures who used the adjective 'Irish' admiringly and not as a synonym for simian clown. All small countries are delighted when their writers win the Nobel Prize or their athletes thrash the giants. When they are given an equal voice in the world of politics, it is heady stuff, and Dublin makes a superhuman effort whenever it comes to hosting the Presidency of the European Union.

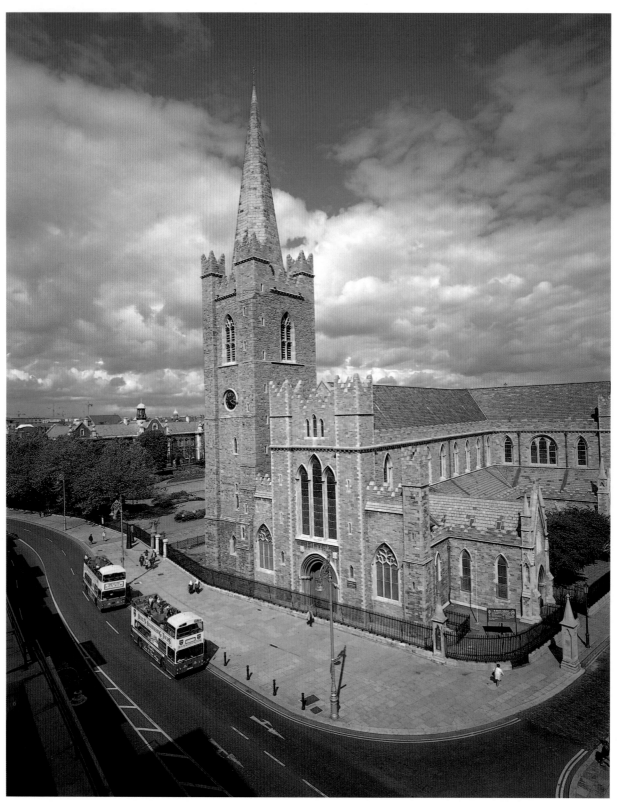

St Patrick's Cathedral

The Hugh Lane Gallery of Modern Art, Parnell Square, was formerly the townhouse of Lord Charlemont, the eighteenth-century Grandee.

Near Dalkey, on the south-eastern shore of Dublin Bay

They came from a land across the sea
And now o'er the western main
Set sail in their good ships gallantly
From the sunny land of Spain.

Salvador de Madariaga, the Spanish philosopher, described the Irish as 'Spaniards who had been left out in the rain' and one sees what he meant. Let a cloud move to reveal the sun, or a stretch come in the evenings, and Dubliners are out on the pavements, celebrating with Mediterranean gusto. 'The most widespread entertainment of the Celts was that derived from story-telling and talking, accompanied by feasting and singing.' Anything is an excuse for a celebration as the 'fighting, dancing, love-making and drollery' of the Donnybrook Fair demonstrated until, in the nineteenth century, 'it forfeited every claim to recognition as a national festivity and in its final stages grew to be a gigantic public nuisance and disgrace.' Before that an indulgent (or blind) visitor noted at Donnybrook that

> . . . not the slightest trace of English brutality is to be perceived; they were more like French people, though their gaiety was mingled with more humour and more genuine good nature; both of which are natural traits of the Irish, and are always doubled by poteen.

When George IV, drunk as a skunk, arrived in 1821, he inspired a huge carnival and was greeted with enormous enthusiasm.

Even when Dublin was at one of its lowest ebbs in 1849, following the abortive rebellion of the Young Irelanders, an epidemic of cholera and the great Famine, a visit by Queen Victoria and Prince Albert was a great success, with illuminations and the electric lighting of Nelson Pillar, cheers and processions and Kingstown Harbour black with people.

Much was read into these presumed outbursts of loyal fervour but, in fact, they are put in perspective by the enthusiasm shown again and again for Daniel O'Connell, or the prize fighter Dan Donnelly's victory parade after he had defeated the English champion, Cooper, in 1815. A million people turned out to greet Pope John Paul II when he came to the Phoenix Park in 1979, but they also came out for boxing champion Barry McGuigan, and for cyclist Stephen Roche, winner of the Tour de France. Possibly the greatest turnout was the welcome given to the Irish football team and their manager, Jack Charlton, when they

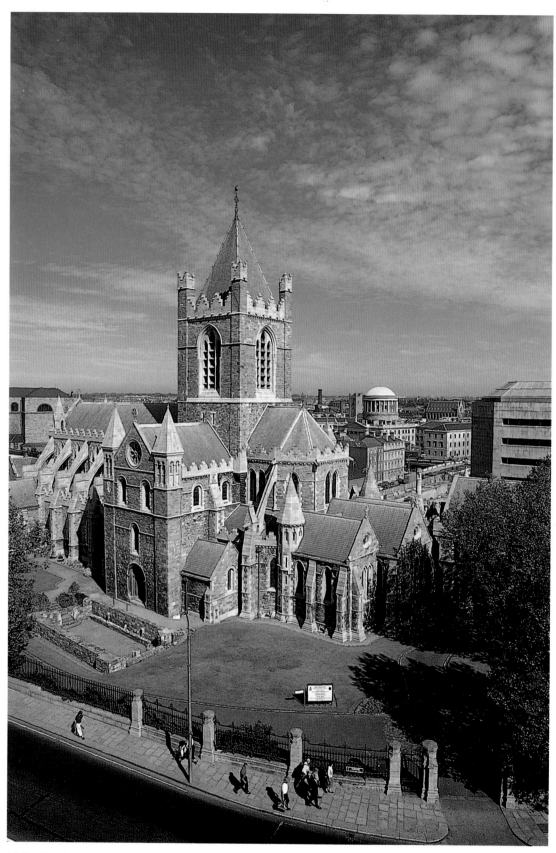

Christ Church Cathedral

Interior of Newman House on St Stephen's Green

returned bloody but unbowed from the World Cup in 1990. When Ireland was taking part in the World Cup, carnival was king.

It is not only the living who are honoured by Dubliners. When Dan Donnelly died, 80,000 people followed the coffin. Every patriot who came home to be buried in Ireland had a guarantee that he would stop the traffic. Brendan Behan's funeral was as good as de Valera's. But then funerals have always been important in Dublin. Paddy Dignam's funeral plays a major role in *Ulysses* and there was a secondary aspect to the Dublin funeral one hundred years ago as Con Curran, a contemporary of Joyce's, explained in his memoirs.

In Dublin, wrote Curran, funerals were a sort of popular pageantry and the long strings of outside cars passing up O'Connell Street to Glasnevin Cemetery on Sundays were a very familiar sight. Not all the passengers, seated three aside on the car, were mourners. One Sunday, a Hungarian visitor was invited to join two passengers on their car in a funeral procession. Not wishing to seem impolite, he went with them and they proceeded cheerfully to the gate of a cemetery but did not enter. Instead, after a respectful pause, they continued their drive for two or three miles to Floods of Finglas and spent a pleasant hour or two there before returning to the city. The afternoon's entertainment cost him nothing.

In the nineteenth century, the secular Irish equivalent of the Semana Santa in Málaga was the Lord Mayor's Parade, with great trade banners which headed each section of the trade unions until the overhead wires of the newly electrified trams made it impossible to carry them. Mounted on floats, these banners advanced slowly like frigates. Twenty feet high, they were corded, tasselled and fringed in green and gold; most were of canvas but some were of silk or poplin. The front usually bore the patron saint of the trade or Erin with harp, round tower and wolfhound. On the reverse, the arms of the trade were supported by allegorical figures of Justice, Concord, Hope, Commerce. Stallions romped for the tanners and saddlers. Eagles, pheasants and rabbits symbolised the poulterers. St Luke could be seen painting the Blessed Virgin. The carpenters' St Joseph wielded his chisel and mallet. The butchers were represented by an Agnus Dei bearing a cross, the shoemakers by St Crispin. In Daniel O'Connell's day there were *tableaux vivants*, Adam and Eve in flesh-coloured tights with a big apple tree standing in a hogshead. St Patrick's Day (17 March) has tried to recapture some of this gaiety, but without great success. March is not a marching month. In the last few years, however, a new Dublin festival has erupted, 16 June, the feast of Saints Molly and Poldy, Bloomsday, which is beginning to spill over into the surrounding weeks.

Dubliners are pleasure mad (the Spanish strain again). Once they flocked to the opera and music-hall. For fifty years there were longer queues for the main cinemas than you

Bloomsday visit to the Joyce Tower. The sign for the adjacent Forty Foot bathing place is frequently ignored these days.

The rickshaw is the latest form of designer transport in the city.

Mulligans of Poolbeg Street, one of Dublin's most famous pubs

Doheny and Nesbitt on Baggot Street is one of Dublin's best known and best loved pubs.

The Café en Seine in Dawson Street is one of the city's most fashionable venues.

At Dublin Horse Show. This young man entered the competition for best hat on Ladies Day — and won!

At the King's Inns

68

would find outside a Moscow bakery. Lately, Dublin's night-clubs have been a stalking ground for international gossip columnists and, all in all, this is a city where people refuse to go to bed early. Every variation of music is available. Once pub windows were impenetrable — those inside did not want to look out and those outside could not look in. Now plate glass windows flaunt the *jeunesse dorée*, packed like sardines, illuminated and unashamed.

I will live in Ringsend
With a red-headed whore,
And the fanlight gone in
Where it lights the halldoor;
And listen each night
For her querulous shout,
As at last she streels in
And the pubs empty out.

The student of Dublin has no shortage of matter on which to reflect. The Dublin pram, for example, whose place in the city's life is summarised in the instruction, 'Maisie, will you lift the babby up and let the lady see the fish!' The Dublin pram in its protean variety and its Lon Chaney talent for disguise is worthy of a doctoral thesis.

Another fruitful field of enquiry would be a study of those people about whom Dubliners tell stories. They are people who have earned a respect that is not given to the street characters. These folk heroes of Dublin have counted for something in the worlds of medicine, science, law, literature, politics, religion, but it is not the finer points of their callings or even their success (for often they were worldly failures) but their nature, their generous response to life's challenges and something that they added to the city that gives them their status.

Perhaps the simple explanation is that they are all the sort of person with whom you would not mind having a drink!

Tom Moore did well for himself and mixed with royalty. Anyone of us could have ended up like poor Mangan with his false teeth and flax wig. Did you know that Peg Woffington started out selling apples and oranges and ended up the toast of London? George Moore made fun of everyone even himself. Sean O'Casey got the dirty end of the stick from those stuck up know-alls in the Abbey. Big Jim

The sculpture stands beside the Conrad Hotel on Earlsfort Terrace.

The wall

The statue of George Bernard Shaw stands outside the National Gallery of Ireland, which he endowed so generously.

Larkin was the only friend of the working man and stood up to the 'Tramway Tyrant', William Martin Murphy, and the Church in 1913. John McCormack beat James Joyce at the Feis Ceoil and lost all his money on the horses. 'The true redeemer of bel canto', they called him. Dracula came from Fairview. He was invented by Bram Stoker. Flann O'Brien could be a wicked little bugger if you riz him but, by God, he was a demon for the repartee. Richard Brinsley Sheridan, when his theatre was burning down in London, he poured himself a drink and told his pals, 'A man is entitled to a sherry by his own fire.' And George Bernard Shaw, he didn't believe in God or devil but he put the fear of God into the philistines. Fair does to Dublin, they put on *The Shewing-up of Blanco Posnet* when the Lord Chamberlain wouldn't allow it over in London.

How otherwise can you explain the common espousal of Swift, Mangan, Emmet, Collins, Connolly, Larkin, Gogarty, Matt Talbot, R. M. Smyllie of *The Irish Times*, Lord and Lady Longford of the Gate Theatre, Alfie Byrne, the Lord Mayor, Maureen Potter and Noel Purcell, Dr Collis, MacLiammmóir and Edwards, while native or adopted sons like Edward Carson and Éamon de Valera never rhyme in the mind with Dublin?

Nowadays all the city can offer are 'celebrities'.

And up the back garden
The sound comes to me
Of the lapsing, unsoilable,
Whispering sea.

In Dublin people look and are looked at. It is hard to imagine someone falling on the footpath in Dublin and being left to lie there. At the end of the second millennium, it remains a city on a human scale with a lot of sky on display. To savour Dublin fully, one must sit in 'the Green' at lunchtime on a sunny day. Face the entrances from Merrion Row, Leeson Street and Harcourt Street and witness a living cyclorama. Who are these actors walking on to that open stage and disappearing across the little bridge into the wings behind? Some stride, some shuffle, some swing. Are they diplomats from Iveagh House? Bankers or musicians from Earlsfort Terrace? Medical students from the Royal College of Surgeons? Tourists from Milwaukee, Tokyo or Sydney? Could the girl with the little hatbox be a Super Model in the making? Doesn't that pretty punk sell fruit and vegetables in Camden Street? The navy-blue trousers worn by those healthy hooligans, girls and boys, identify them as trainee gardaí (police officers) from Harcourt Street.

In Temple Bar

Temple Bar interior

Crossing the Ha`penny Bridge in the rain

Newman House interior

Lately a comedian remarked, 'Isn't it wonderful? If you go into Dublin pubs, you will meet playwrights, novelists and poets in every one. In other countries, they would call them drunks. . . .'

Nowadays a young man or woman is more likely to have a filmscript in his or her briefcase than the plot of an unwritten novel in (usually) their head. Poetry will never leave Dublin, but much of the energy that went into verse is now directed to performing one's own songs at gigs in singing pubs.

Our galleries and museums cannot compete with Vienna or St Petersburg. On the other hand, you can see everything they have to offer before the exhibits begin to blur together before your eyes. In some cases, like the Irish Museum of Modern Art up at the Royal Hospital Kilmainham, the setting *vaut le détour* (pity about the contents).

As in all things, there are fashionable and unfashionable artists. At present, there is a tendency to neglect not only those poets, novelists and playwrights like Denis Johnston, Seán O'Faolain, Liam O'Flaherty, Denis Devlin, Brian Coffey, Austin Clarke, Thomas Kinsella and Lennox Robinson, whose popular growth was stunted in the shade of the giants (not to speak of exotic blooms like Annie M. P. Smithson), but some important contemporary writers. Roddy Doyle may be as famous as Bono but Dermot Bolger has ploughed the Finglas fields in a similar vein; Adrian Kenny has explained the lives of first-generation Dubliners in Jesuit schools and comfortable suburbs; Philip Casey has nursed to unbearable life an underworld frozen on the Ha'penny Bridge.

> *I wandered north, and I wandered south*
> *By Golden Lane and Patrick's Close,*
> *The Coombe, Smithfield and Stoneybatter,*
> *Back to Napper Tandy's house.*
> *Old age has laid its hand upon me*
> *Cold as a fire of ashy coal —*
> *And where is the lovely Spanish Lady*
> *That maid so neat about the sole?*

One of a deafening *tertulia* of students chattering outside HMV in Grafton Street like a swarm of Iberian starlings, that's where she is.

As the great Russian writers came out from under Gogol's 'Overcoat', preconceptions about Dublin start with James Malton's *Picturesque and Descriptive Views of Dublin*,

Scenes in Temple Bar. The whole area has been transformed from a neglected and dilapidated warren of narrow streets into the vibrant centre of Dublin's burgeoning arts community.

The corner of Cope Street, the shadow of the giant Central Bank

Temple Bar has some of the most exciting and stylish architecture in the city.

Street scene in the area of Guinness's Brewery

those aquatint records of the portico of Parliament House, Dublin Castle, Trinity College, the Provost's House, 1 Grafton Street ('the most beautiful interior in Dublin'), St Patrick's, the Tholsel, the Royal Infirmary and St Catherine's Church among others. They are all there, the true lodestar, what Dublin must measure itself against. They are tranquil and stately. The most agitated is the Marine School looking up the Liffey, a reminder that Dublin is the gateway to an island and that wind and rain and stormy seas have always lain between Dublin and much that was dear to it. The good news is that the lack of a fair wind delayed Oliver Cromwell's arrival in 1649 and he was thoroughly seasick by the time he arrived to stop the people of Dublin 'profaning, swearing, drinking, cursing, which were said to be the daily practice of the place'.

When you walk through a house in which you have lived for most of your life, your main focus of interest is not on the proportions of the rooms, the harshness of its skyline or the purity of its chimneys. It is on the corner of the stairs where you read *Treasure Island*, the carving of the turkey at Christmas, the telephone through which good and bad news came impartially, the mirror in which ghosts are reflected. Dublin is no different. Personal and historical memories coat its buildings as surely as coal dust and diesel fumes, but the former cannot be cleaned off by high-speed sprays behind sheets of canvas.

In some cases, the personal is more immediate than the historical and then buildings and places achieve the status of Dublin institutions: Bewley's Oriental Café, the Gate Theatre, the Gaiety, Guinness's Brewery, the Royal Dublin Society in Ballsbridge and its annual Horse Show, the Pro Cathedral and the Palestrina Choir, Whitefriar's Church in Aungier Street with its medieval statue of Our Lady of Dublin, the Black Church, the 'Pepper Canister' in Upper Mount Street, Marsh's Library, Moore Street, Merrion Square, the banks of the Dodder, the Furry Glen in the Phoenix Park, and (for some) the Bridewell and Mountjoy Jail.

The Abbey Theatre, the Phoenix Park — the largest enclosed park in Europe — and the General Post Office, have an important role in the memories of individuals, but they have also been players in the Story of Ireland and their ghosts are as often public as private. Here, the Rotunda is the quintessential hybrid: Pleasure Gardens, theatre, cinema, dance-hall and, primarily, Dr Mosse's Lying in Hospital, of whose second Master it was said,

Sir Fielding Ould is made a knight
He should have been a Lord by right,
For then the ladies' cry would be,
'O Lord, good Lord, deliver me'

Shadows in the foyer of the Irish Film Centre

Early morning scene in the Phoenix Park

In an increasingly secular city, sport is replacing religion in many ways and, for those who still cherish Catholic Gaelic Ireland, it is comforting to learn that, following an international rugby match at Lansdowne Road, there are many more requests for morning-after pills than after an All-Ireland hurling or Gaelic football final at Croke Park.

The market makers claim that Ireland is in the throes of a cultural renaissance, that Irish plastic artists now show their work as a matter of course at contemporary art biennials as far apart as Venice and São Paulo, and that writers, musicians (classical and popular), painters, sculptors, film-makers and actors are showing new confidence about entering on to a larger stage. There is certainly a shift towards looking at the arts as an industry rather than as an introspective pastime in an ivory tower, and the artists are receiving wider recognition. Dublin has at least thirty commercial art galleries. This talk of culture renaissance is all very fine but only if renaissance means exactly what it says. It is the re-birth of an old tradition, not the invention of something *ex nihilo*.

'The Welsh . . . are the only nation in the world that has produced no graphic or plastic art, no architecture, no drama. They just sing . . . and blow down wind instruments of plated silver.' The equivalent of this modest pronouncement which Evelyn Waugh put in the mouth of the headmaster in his novel *Decline and Fall*, is set out repeatedly in serious works about Ireland: 'Because of her history, Irish talent has been primarily oral.' A crass generalisation like this ignores the lunulae, earrings, torcs, collars, gorgets, shields, swords, chalices and crosses in bronze and gold to be seen in the National Museum, the Book of Kells in Trinity College, the Book of Durrow, the stone gods and crosses, the church builders. It passes over the 160 named painters and the mass of unattributed work of the Irish School in the *Summary Catalogue of Paintings of the National Gallery of Ireland*, and the Irish paintings in the Municipal Gallery and the modern galleries. It forgets the long tradition of Irish music. By way of excuse, we could agree that the painters, sculptors, musicians and builders, who were always here, were renationalised by the patrons who paid them. The description by English media of natives of Thomas Street or Rathmines as the 'British' actor, film director, golfer, footballer or athlete has by now acquired the patina of a well-worn family joke.

'If there is an Irish cultural renaissance, then Temple Bar in Dublin would be its Florence.' Few things change as quickly as slang but the disyllabic 'Dortwords' 'coo-ul' and 'deadly' are still current in Dublin, which is now a very cool city, and, other than the night-clubs with their descendants of the Dublin 'charlies' — the hair-gelled bouncers — the coolest place is Temple Bar.

This area between Dame Street and Wellington Quay, absorbing the forecourt of the Central Bank, was prosperous in the eighteenth century, with shops, workshops and warehouses. Local music-halls and the Stock Exchange kept it going until the end of World War II. The area declined then and, while waiting to become a bus station, was home to a variety of alternative small businesses, collectives and hip lifestyles. Nicknamed Dublin's Left Bank, it is more than post-adolescents nursing pints on the pavement. The Irish Film Centre and the Project Theatre are here. There are painting, sculpture and photographic

Bray Head in the mist

Killiney Bay, with Bray Head in the distance

Howth Harbour and Ireland's Eye

studio facilities, recording studios, a multi-media centre, exhibition space, archives, training centres, performances and bars.

As an older generation would say, 'Yiz have no excuse now!'

Yes, Dublin is a historical city. Yes, although its size makes the eastern half of the country top heavy, it is a small and intimate city. But it is not a provincial city any more.

Whatever relics of old Ireland cling like ivy to the ruined Round Tower on which Éire is supporting herself, or nestle like fleas in her wolfhound's hide, they do not float down the Liffey any more. Michael Jackson means more to the child gyrating on the street corner than Cuchullain or St Martin de Porres. The sinking ship deserted the rats when Paddy O'Brien left McDaid's for Grogan's in South William Street; and the literary tourist who goes to Harry Street to be insulted by a genius will find young persons with brief-cases who read Terry Pratchett, if they read at all.

It is not only the security men outside the great stores who whisper to each other on their walkie-talkies. Emigration and electronics have transformed life. Once the dream was escape to the never-never land glamourised by Hollywood or an intellectual Eden in Paris, Madrid or Moscow. 'Abroad' was something to drool about over one's pint. Today, in back alleys and shady snugs, at the Dog Races in Harold's Cross, old Dublin may linger on, but, out in the open, Abroad has come to town and is sipping cappuccino at Café en Seine in Dawson Street. The clothes, the talk, the amusements are cosmopolitan. Dublin is a European city with North American attachments.

Howth Harbour

The great necropolis of Glasnevin Cemetery, with the Daniel O'Connell memorial round tower in the background

Sunset over the Liffey, with the dome of the Custom House on the left and the Irish Life Centre on the right

The most telling metaphor of this new Dublin has been the reopening of a true Dublin institution, the Clarence Hotel on Wellington Quay. One hundred and forty years old, decorated in Arts and Crafts style at the turn of the nineteenth century, this solid old hotel was frequented by members of the legal profession, commercial travellers and farmers up from the country. It was a place where parish priests took their mothers to dinner and, when they brought your plate, the meat and floury potatoes were falling off the sides. Now, at a cost of over £7 million, two rock stars, Bono and The Edge of U2, and impresario Harry Crosbie of the Point Depot, have refurbished it and turned it into a 'boutique hotel with the gorgeous simplicity that only comes from buying the best'.

Joyce's 'commodious *vicus*' is, in fact, past and future meeting; and some of those tasting a frozen dacquiri in the Clarence's bar, The Kitchen, may remember with sadness Micheál MacLiammóir as an actor/Robert Emmet looking down on Dublin and reciting the last lines of Denis Johnston's play, *The Old Lady Says 'No!'*:

> *Strumpet City in the sunset*
> *Suckling the bastard brats of Scot, of Englishry, of Huguenot,*
> *Brave sons breaking from the womb, wild sons fleeing from their Mother*
> *Wilful City of savage dreamers*
> *So old, so sick with memories!*
> *Old Mother;*
> *Some they say are damned*
> *But you, I think, one day will walk the streets of Paradise*
> *Head high, and unashamed.*

For the final word on Dublin, one must paraphrase Oscar Wilde: 'It is exquisite and it leaves one unsatisfied. What more could one want?'